THE HAPHAZARD BOOK OF ILLUSTRATIONS

BY

Michael W. Mosley

I dedicate this book to family, friends, God, and Nena—the lady that I love.

I sincerely hope that the reader finds this book entertaining and inspiring. God bless.

Archery has long been a sport that people have enjoyed. For many centuries, man has hunted and taken wild game with bows and arrows. I know of one man who killed over 75 deer with one early make of compound bow that he bought back in the early 1970's. He also killed over 20 deer with recurve bows. One fellow in Alabama has been something of a legend in the bow hunting community. He has killed probably 450-500 deer with his bows while shooting broad heads that he specially designs. I have never killed a deer while bow hunting, but came very close to shooting a deer one time with a bow and arrow. The arrow went flying through the hair of the animal, but didn't hit the animal—ha! I have been a pretty good shot with a bow at targets, but I was up in a tree stand and hadn't had much practice shooting from a tree stand with a bow. It definitely is different from shooting at a target while you are standing on the ground. I have shot alligator gars, buffalo fish, and other fish that are typically considered trash fish, with a bow and arrow. Usually it was at night and my uncle and I shined a Q-Beam light into the water to illuminate the fish so that we could get a shot at one. That is some fun with a bow and arrow, let me tell you. Fun and challenging. Because of the refraction error of the water, you have to shoot a little below where it appears that the fish is located in order to hit it with the arrow. Not every arrow that flew hit the target. That's the challenging part. Loads of fun can be had by going bow fishing either in the night or in the day time. Fun. Fun. Fun. That's what bow fishing is.

The automobile has been a huge blessing for the world as far as transportation goes. Before the automobile came into being, mankind had to walk, ride on the backs of animals such as the horse, the mule, the camel, or the elephant, according to what area of the world he or she was located in. Men and women rode bicycles and other crude conveyances before the automobile came along. Of course, there was the trains that traveled the tracks and boats and ships that traveled the water, but for travel across the land, the automobile was a blessing of an improvement over bumping up and down on the back of a horse or other critter. Cars and trucks have revolutionized the world as far as land travel goes. Nearly every household in America has at least one or two cars sitting in the driveway or out on the road heading somewhere. Many folks enjoy just getting out of the house to ride around and see what they can see on a road trip, etc. And there are car clubs where folks come to see the older classic automobiles from days gone by. And there are sports such as drag racing and stock car racing and other types of automobile racing which spectators pay premium prices to watch in huge arenas while sitting in stands eating popcorn and guzzling down their favorite soft drinks. Yes, the automobile is a great addition to the world as we know it. So, buckle your seat belts and enjoy the ride.

Mortar and Pestle. The mortar and pestle is used to mix ingredients that are combined to be used as medicine. These tools have been a blessing as far as mixing medical compounds goes. Medicine would not be the same without this necessary tool.

Ape Man, Big Foot, Yeti, Sasquatch, or whatever you choose to call it---and I do mean IT! Who knows what the mysterious beast is. Most researchers think that it is a primitive and as of yet, un-evolved creature and could be more than one type of creature that is (or are) very illusive and present in the most dense forests around the world. There seems to be more sightings in America and Canada than anywhere else in the world, but who knows where their home base is? I surely don't know. So, when you are deep in the forest, get that camera ready, and listen intently for the sounds of the creature—

and snap that photo or capture that video so you can post the photo or video on the internet for the

rest of the world to see.

Submarines (Submersible vessels) have been around a long time. For the most part, they have been used for military purposes mostly associated with warfare and monitoring the water for enemy activity. There are submarines in use throughout the world as research vessels. The study of fishes, and other sea life has benefitted from the use of submarines. I have seen submarines that were used for checking on the structural status of bridges and other underwater structures. I have been inside a submarine that was used heavily during WW2. Submarines are propelled through the water by nuclear powered engines in modern times, but the very early models were propelled by human-power in much the same way that a person rides a bicycle. Of course, several people had to pedal it to get it to move about under the water. Several early- day crews even drowned inside some of the vessels. Modern day submarines can stay underwater for months at a time, but the early vessels were not able to stay under very long. Submarines are useful in some ways, and will always be around in one form or another.

The hot air balloon is a unique way to travel through the air. Back in the beginning days of hot air balloon usage, a fire was made in a container so that the smoke could fill the balloon and thus float the balloon upward. Modern versions mostly use gas- burning tanks to fill the balloon with the gas needed to lift the balloon up into the air. During the American Civil War, the smoke-filled balloons were used to fly over enemy troops to spy on them and find out what they were trying to do. Of course, the enemy troops would shoot their rifles at the balloons to try to make it fall to the ground. I paid a small fee one time and was carried up high above a grocery store parking lot by a balloon that was tethered by a long rope. I sometimes hear some horror stories of people who were killed when balloons that they were being carried by hit electrical power lines and exploded. Some of the balloons were carried into trees or towers or other things and the people riding them were killed. These were terrible events, to say the least. Folks have attempted to cross oceans in balloons. Folks have attempted to go up into outer space. Yes, balloons have been used to do some spectacular things. But, it isn't my favorite form of travel. No, I am a little more than just a little bit wary about flying by balloon. But, enjoy if you must. Enjoy if you must. And I hope it works out well for you. Good luck.

The tree. Home to many birds. Shade for those who need to get out of the heat of the sun. Building material for homes, buildings, animal enclosures, boats and ships, etc. Paper is made from wood fibers combined with certain chemicals and processed. Children all over the world have climbed trees and played in them. Men in wars have climbed up trees so that they could spy on the enemy troops or shoot their sniper rifles from their high perch. Men have built bridges out of logs and lumber has been cut out of trees. Airplanes have been built out of wood that came from trees. Animals make their homes or hide in the hollow trunks of trees. Fruits are harvested from trees. Trees are a very important part of the world. A very important part. And I am thankful for the trees. Very thankful.

The lamp. Lamps of all sorts have been used by people over the centuries. Back in the earliest of times (What I refer to as The bible days: Meaning the days just before, during, and just after Jesus Christ was still walking around and doing his ministry on earth), the lamps were simpler and had a wick sticking out of a simple clay vessel. In later years, the basic lamp was changed in some ways, but it still is basically a wick that is sticking out of some type of vessel that holds oil or fuel. Kerosene is the most common type of lamp oil in modern times. Miners used Carbide Lamps: A lamp that ran off carbide gas. The gas was made by mixing calcium carbide and water. Coon hunters(Raccoon) used the lights and cave explorers used them. Carbide lamps had a smell to them that wasn't exactly pleasant. These lights weren't as bright as more modern kerosene lamps or the battery-powered lamps. Lamps were used by the railroad workers over the years and lamps were used onboard the whaling ships and other ships over the last couple of centuries. There has always been a need for light in the dark of night or in underground places where the light of day never shines. Of course, the most common light that people use in modern times is the flashlight. Flashlights of many types now exist and come in handy at night. But the common kerosene lamp or lantern still is used by folks today and most likely always will be used as long as people venture out into the dark places.

The bicycle is one of the most common modes of transportation in the world. Most of the more crowded areas of the world make heavy use of bicycles as their means of transportation. China, Viet Nam, and many other countries are literally covered with bicycle-riding people who don't own a motorized vehicle of any kind. In the USA, many children have a bicycle as their first mode of transportation (Of course, their parents usually drive a car or truck) and they ride their bicycle all around within short distances of their home. I remember we (My brother, and cousin, and I) used to ride our bicycles for several miles and back on trips to the swimming hole or other places. We even jumped ramps to emulate the heroic acts of Evel Knievel—ha! And I will never forget on one jump I went over the ramp and sailed through the air and the front wheel fell off and I landed harshly with the front forks jabbed into the ground and I sailed away from the bicycle and landed on the ground. My younger brother and cousin had loosened the nuts that held the wheel on and they began to laugh hysterically. So, I know something about bicycles and their shortcomings—ha! There is nothing more nice than a good long bicycle ride on a pretty day. So grab your bicycle and go for a ride. It's hardly ever disappointing. Besides the good exercise, there's always something to see along the way. So enjoy.

Canoeing is something that people have done for centuries. The American Indians canoed on rivers and streams as one of their main modes of transportation. White men caught onto the idea and began doing the same. Canoeing is a peaceful way of getting to a destination down river from where you are when you start your journey. In modern times, canoeing is more often a form of recreation and enjoyment. Many vacationers and summer camp attenders canoe along on the rivers and streams just for the fun of it and for being out in nature. I used to own a 13.5' canoe that I used to paddle down the streams with friends. I remember one time as I made my way down a narrow body of water, my friend grabbed ahold of a tree limb as we passed it and the canoe fell over and both of us and all of our stuff went into the water. I was aggravated about it because I lost a knife that cost about 75 dollars if you bought it new. I dove down a couple times to try to find it, but couldn't locate it in the deep murky water. I don't even remember that young fellow's name, but I remember losing that 75 dollar knife..ha! A good friend (Whom I play guitar with sometimes) and I went on a four day canoeing trip one time. We camped out two nights, met some crazy- acting people on the river who were drinking and just a tad over influenced by the liquid that they had been engulfing. Oh, they were friendly to us, but just a tad on the wobbly-bobbly side, if you know what I mean.

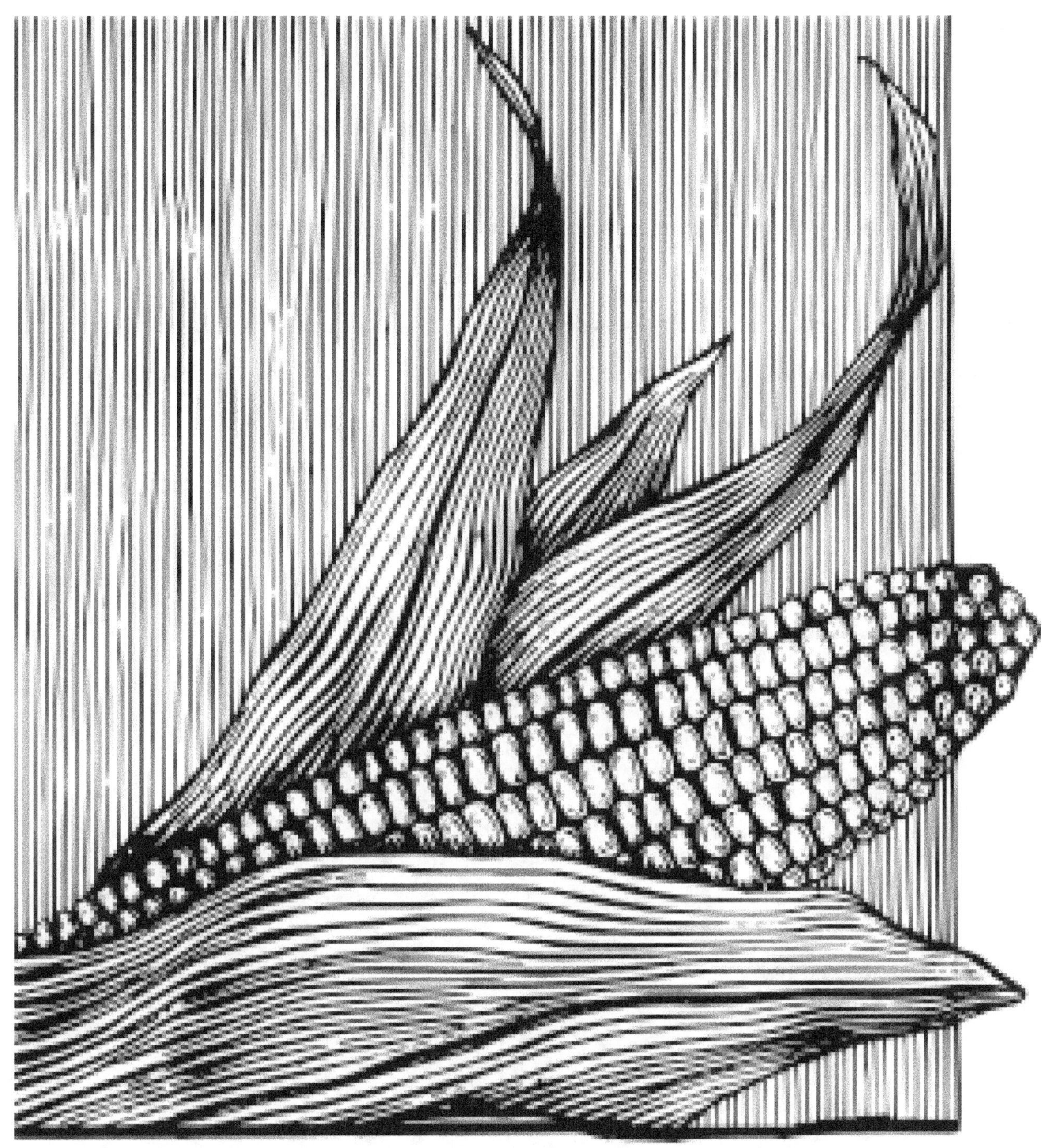

Corn. The Indians called it maize. Whatever you choose to call it, it is a wonderful food when fixed just right. Historians say that the Indians introduced maize to the pilgrims who settled at Plymouth Plantation . And they say that the first Thanks Giving was in 1621 and it was a 3-day festival of hunting, cooking, and had about 90 Native Americans and 53 English Pilgrims in attendance. Corn/maize was one of the foods that was eaten at that festival of Thanksgiving for the first successful harvest.

Corn has been ground into smaller parts to make corn meal, grits, and corn bread. I like eating corn bread with lima beans, boiled cabbage, and other vegetables. On a cold winter day, a bowl of hot soup or stew and some corn bread really makes you feel comfortable and satisfied. I make the old-style pone bread on the griddle pan. Wow, that's good with beans, cabbage, stew, or soups. Some folks might call what I make on the griddle pan "Hoe Cakes." But I call it pone bread. Whatever you call it, it is good as gold. Especially when you are hungry. One way that I like to eat corn is wrapped in tin foil with herbs and spices and butter inside the tin foil. When that corn gets done, it is like magic to the taste buds. And I always make sure to add some kernel corn to my beef stew or beef soups. It is a thing of beauty. A wonderful thing of beauty. Corn is an amazing food. Simply amazing.

Helicopters are very important. The first helicopters were created to be used by the military. They were used heavily during the Korean Conflict and the Vietnam War. Some helicopters are very large and can carry tons of military equipment such as jeeps, heavy artillery, and soldiers. Helicopters have been used for hauling logs, equipment, and crew men in the forests of the world. Helicopters have been used to carry badly- injured people to hospitals miles away from the scene of the accident. Some helicopters are in use to carry sight-seers above the Grand Canyon, and other scenic places in the world. Helicopters are used to carry water and fire-repelling chemicals to where fires are raging in the forests. Some helicopters are in use by scientists all over the world to help them to see certain aspects of nature such as animal migrations and locations of wolf packs, etc. Photographers sometimes charter helicopter pilots to take them above scenic areas so that they can photograph from a high elevation. Some animal researchers ride in helicopters so that they can shoot animals with a dart to put the animal to sleep for a short while so that researchers can place tags or tracking devices on the animal. And sometimes an animal must be put asleep so that a veterinarian can perform some life-saving task to help the animal. Helicopters are used to track criminals by police departments and sometimes the best way to catch a criminal who is running away from the police is to follow them with a helicopter. Many suspects have been caught with the help of a pilot flying a helicopter above what is going on. Many folks have been rescued by being lifted out of the water, from canyons, from floods, and other Places and situations. So, you see, a helicopter can be a very useful thing in many situations.

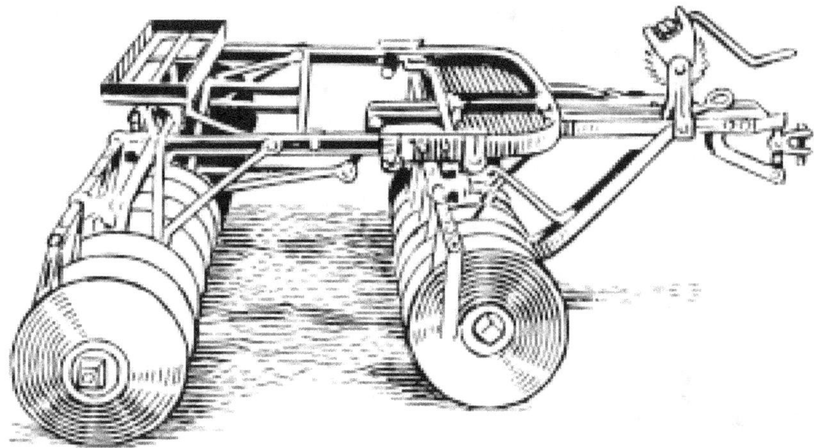

The disc (disk) or harrow. Most farmers just call it a disc. This piece of equipment is pulled behind a tractor to break up the soil down to several inches so that it will be ready to be planted with crops. The ground would be too hard for the plants to grow easily if it weren't disc'd (disked) or harrowed. I have ridden on tractors as a young boy as my grandfather disked the garden or field. Dust would fly all about as the tractor pulled the disc through the dry ground. But it was and still is a very necessary part of farming the land. My stepdad had a lawn tractor with a small disc he disked his garden plot with. And a larger one he pulled with his medium-sized tractor. One of my paternal grandmother's brothers was a farmer and he rode around in a large tractor that had an air-conditioned cab and the disc that he pulled with that tractor was a very wide affair that could disc many rows at a time. Now, that's the way to go…ha! We never had such luxuries on the tractors that my granddaddy or my step daddy used. You had to endure the heat and the dust and keep to the task regardless of these pesky inconveniences. We used tractors to pull up saplings that my granddaddy didn't want on the land, and we used tractors to pull logs and poles around whenever we needed to move them. And on occasions, we used tractors to pull vehicles out of mudholes whenever someone got stuck in them. And a few times over the years, we went on hayrides. We would talk and laugh and have a good ol' time while the fellow on the tractor pulled us around. What fun we had doing that. And there were always some cute girls that we enjoyed kidding and admiring. Oh yeah, those were some really- fun times. So, you see, tractors are useful pieces of equipment for sure. And sometimes a means of having a little fun, as in the case of the tractors pulling those hay-filled wagons for us to ride. And disc (disk) harrows are very useful pieces of farming equipment. Without them farming would be a lot less productive.

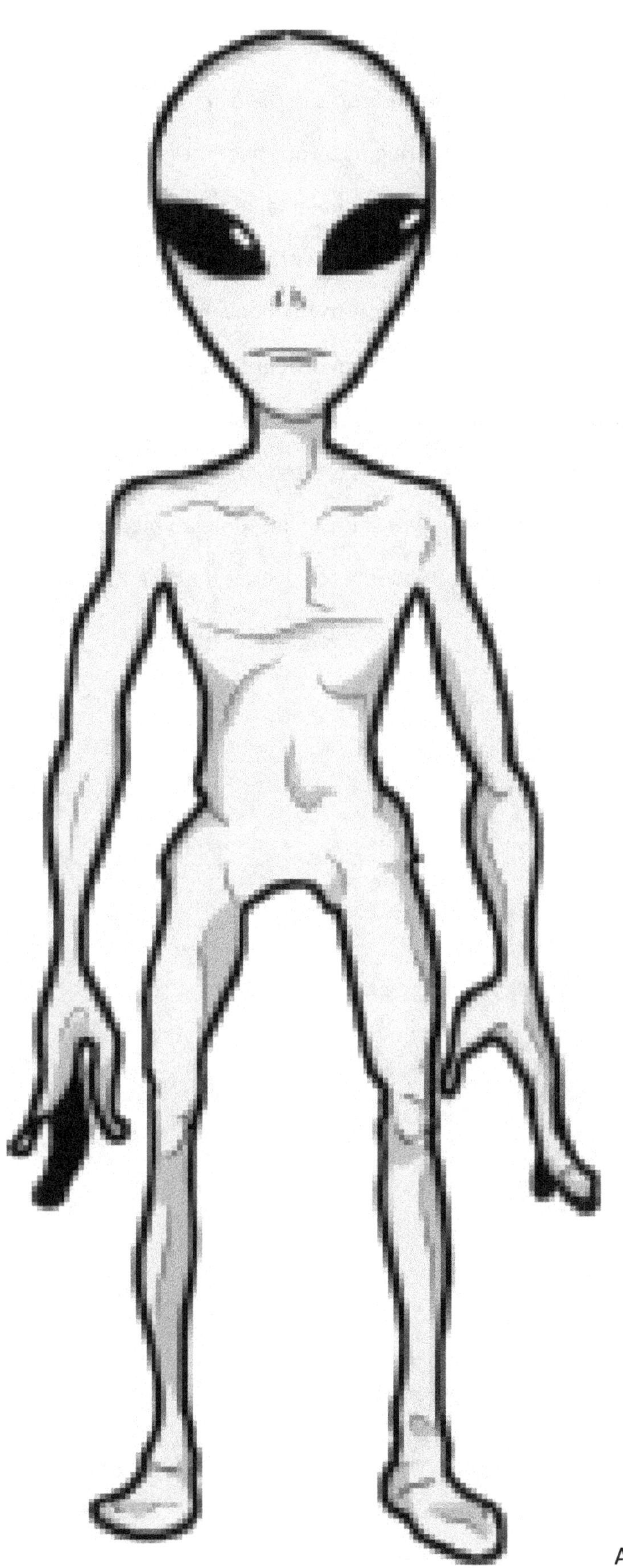

Aliens, UFO's, Little Green Men, whatever you

choose to call them, many folks believe that they exist and some say that they have encountered the creatures from other worlds beyond our galaxy. They say that the creatures come from other worlds and have made strides to come to earth to study humans and to bring us a variety of messages and technologies very foreign to our own. Are they real? I have no clue, but I have talked to people who say that they have seen strange UFO's in the sky. Strange lights zipping across the sky swifter than any known aircraft could manage to do. Hovering lights that suddenly zip off to the heavens like nothing else could do. And I know of some cases where people claim to have been brought aboard the space crafts and creatures examined them for some unknown purpose. And some folks have claimed that an alien had embedded some kind of device in their body. Some say this is a tracking device. I have had no such experiences and don't want them either…ha! I've never seen a UFO, unless you can count the "Unidentified Frying Object" in somebody's frying pan…ha! But some folks insist that the little green men do indeed exist. I don't know, maybe they do, maybe they don't. Who knows? Not I. Surely not I.

The house boat has been a very popular way to enjoy being on the river. It is basically a home on the water. Many house boats can be seen tied to the bank on many rivers in America and other places. Most folks who own house boats use them for recreation mostly on the weekends, but some folks live on their house boats. Life is usually simple there, and the cares of the world can be forgotten temporarily while looking out across the water and maybe casting a line out to see if you can catch a fish. Most folks cook on barbecue grills, but some have electrical outlets and use the same type of electrical appliances that most folks have in their homes. And many folks have a TV and watch their favorite shows while they aren't riding in their boat or fishing or swimming, etc. My family owns a pretty decent house boat with electrical appliances, restroom, and basically the same conveniences that an apartment would have. I've spent a few nights in it and have endured loud snoring (From kin folks), rocking up and down when the weather is rough and the water is wavy, and some scary lightning striking weather that'd scare the crap out of anyone with any sense in their head….ha! But, for the most part, I have enjoyed being able to spend time on the family house boat. And we have had some pretty good meals on the house boat that included grilled chicken, burgers, and grilled corn on the cob. Yummy! That's some really good eating. And it seemed to be even better when eaten down on the houseboat with kin folks, friends, and even a pet or two…ha! Oh yes, the house boat is a pretty good place to be when you want to forget about your cares and just enjoy a day or two of being down on the river and not stuck at home doing "The same ol' same ol'" as some folks like to say.

Fishing. The illustration above shows some beaded bait being used to attract the fish, but many types of baits have been used to attract fish over the centuries. Primitive me and women used sticks/clubs to hit a fish in the water to kill it or stun it enough to be able to grab the fish. Some folks in ancient times threw spears at fish and sometimes were able to kill them that way. Some folks made traps to catch the fish. The traps were usually primitive contraptions made of natural materials such as sticks driven into the ground and netting made of tied pieces of cord that they made from various materials readily at hand. For thousands of years men and women have caught fish by setting out nets (Or casting them) and waiting for the fish to enter the nets and get caught in them. This is one of the most productive methods of fishing. But, sadly, it has been overdone so much that many species of fish have been almost depleted in the oceans of the world. It would be a terrible and sad thing for many fishes to go extinct, so better management of the fishing industry may be in order. We need to preserve our fish species as much as we can so that the fishes of the world can regain population and thrive.

For salt water fishing, folks fish with live shrimp, dead shrimp, dead squid, worms of various types, artificial worms, live worms, cut bait (Cut up mullet, for example), shad, cigar minnows, small crabs, artificial crabs, and other baits.

In fresh water, most folks use wiggler worms, night crawlers, crickets (Both alive and artificial), and all sorts of artificial baits like plastic worms and lizards, buzz baits, spinner baits, fishing plugs of many types. The sport of fishing is a huge industry and fishing is one of the most popular activities in the world and surely in America. One method of getting fish is gigging. In the summer months, many folks like to wade the shallows at night with a bright light of some kind and a sharp gig on the end of a pole. Well actually, the pole is a part of the gig, but the part I call the gig is the sharp rod or more than one rod that sticks out from the pole. These can be barbed or barbless. I've never gigged a flounder, but I have gigged crabs and other fish on flounder gigging trips that I went on when I was a teenager. It was great fun wading around and seeing cigar fish, crabs, and other creatures in the lit- up water. I made a pair of floundering lights and some gigs earlier this summer, but had some skin cancer issues and was unable to try my luck with them. Maybe next season I will wade the water and gig a flounder for the first time. Maybe. So, you see, many baits and methods have been used to catch fish. And fishing will surely always be one of the world's most popular pastimes. But I doubt commercial fishermen/or women, call it a pastime. For them, it is a way of life.

The wild boar. This animal species has caused much damage of the land in many states in the U.S.A.
these creatures can be very mean and dangerous. I've heard about men getting chased up trees and
some unlucky folks have been attacked by them and the wounds that their large tusks created were very
severe. These tusks can be very sharp and can split a person's flesh wide open. Some very nasty wounds
have been inflicted on folks who were hunting or otherwise in the woods where these creatures tend to
abide. People go into the forest and wait for the wild boars or the female hogs to come walking by. And
they (The hunter or hunters) try to take a shot before the creature or creatures make an escape into
the denseness of the forest. The creatures are overabundant in the forests adjoining rivers and swamps.
They root up the ground and eat vegetation and are very destructive to the areas that they inhabit.
My brother and cousins have shot wild hogs and the meat is very good tasting when prepared right. A
thing to remember, is that the females are more likely to taste better because the boar hogs have glands
that can make the meat taste bad unless you know how to take care of the hog in such a way that it will
have better tasting meat. Some folks say that if you catch wild hogs and put them in a pen and feed
them with corn for a while, it will make the meat of the animal taste much better whenever the animal
is butchered and cooked.

Owls are very interesting creatures. Much has been written about these stealthy hunters. They hunt for rodents of various types, rabbits, and other small creatures. The owl can silently swoop down upon an unsuspecting creature before the creature even realizes what has happened. Owls have been known to be mysterious creatures and have been thought of as magical and even evil. Actuality, I think that owls are just members of the animal kingdom and part of God's creation on earth that are simply doing what they were created to do. They must survive somehow, and so they fly around and hunt for other creatures to eat. It's just the way it is. It is the way of life for these creatures. They are more apt to be night hunters, but owls are also known to hunt in the day time. Some owls live in hollow trees and others such as barn owls make their nest in old barns and such structures. The barn owls sit on a perch in a barn and silently scan the barn with their keen eye sight for any movement such as a mouse or rat moving around. I doubt that a barn owl has to worry about getting enough to eat in a barn where sacks of feed and corn are sitting around. Mice and Rats love such places and stick around to eat whatever feed or grains they can get ahold of. So, a barn owl naturally has plenty of these creatures to eat. Owls are associated with the traditions of Halloween. Scientists have studied these creatures to see how they manage to fly so silently through the air, and how they dive down upon their prey so swiftly. Owls are very interesting creatures, to say the least.

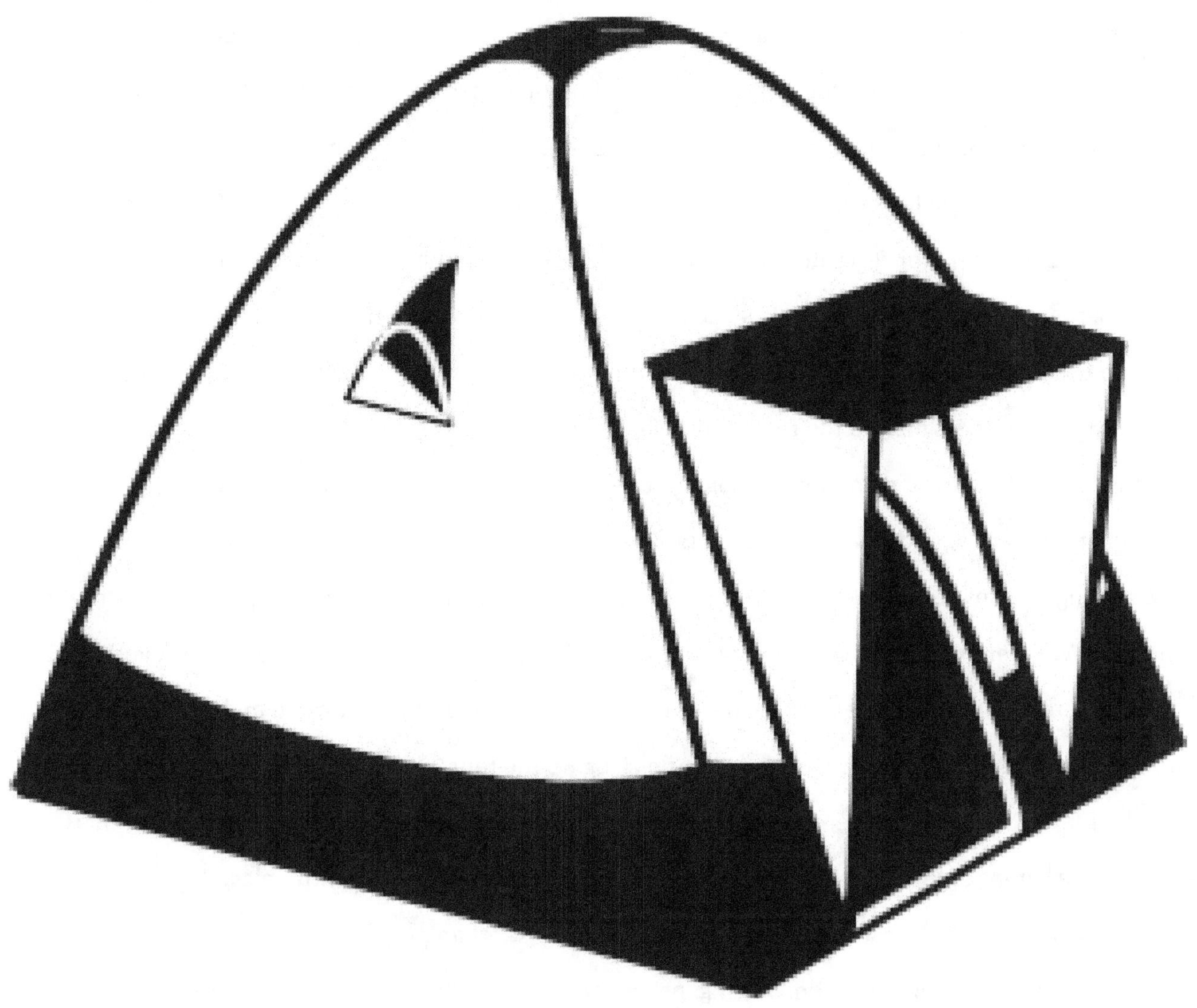

Tents have been in use for thousands of years. Tents are mentioned in the books of the bible. The tribes of Israel lived in tents and whenever they had to move from one place to another, they would take down their tents and take them with them on their journey to their destination. During the American Civil War, and most likely during many other military campaigns, the saying, "Strike the tents." Meant to dismantle or take down the tents. "Strike the camp", meant to begin dismantling the whole camp so that everything could be moved to another location. In ancient times, the Hebrews lived a nomadic life much like today's Bedouins and the tents that they lived in were made from black goat hair that was spun into panels that were sewn or woven together. The Romans had tents that had leather coverings, and then began to use a hemp canvas type material. The militaries all over the world have used tents for temporary quarters when out in the field. While on bivouac, an American soldier would sleep in a small tent that was made with two halves. One soldier had one half, and another soldier had a half.

When they put the two halves together, it made one tent just big enough for them to stay in during

the night. My dad said that he stayed in one of these tents in Army boot camp. These tents were made

out of canvas material. Most modern tents are made of nylon material. Many types of tents are sold

to folks who use them for recreational purposes. One of my best friends and I stayed in a tent one night

during a down pour and whenever either of us would touch the side of the tent, the water would begin

to seep in and soak us. That was not so fun, but other than that, we had a blast and caught catfish and

cooked them on sticks next to the roaring fire. I remember hearing some spooky sounds and to my

teenage mind, it was some ominous "Booger man" coming to attack us in the night. You never know.

You just never know. And I'll never forget the time on Friday the 13th, when my brother, my cousins, and

I was riding in an old car that my dad was driving down an old dusty road with the surplus army tent on

the back. We were riding along and everything seemed alright, when someone looked back and realized

that the tent had fallen off the back of the vehicle. My dad turned the car around and we high-tailed

it back to where the tent lay in the road. After picking up the tent, we continued to the camping spot,

set the tent up, and had a decent time camping. Tents are even used in extreme conditions, such as

at the base camps of folks climbing Mount Everest, and at the North and South poles. Modern tents,

are typically made of polyester, or nylon. Nylon is a bit lighter than polyester. A lot of the more

affordable tents are made of nylon. Staying inside a tent is safer than sleeping on the ground in a

sleeping bag or under a blanket. For one thing, creatures like snakes and scorpions aren't as likely to

get to you if you are inside a tent with the flaps closed tight. I have heard some tales of campers who

have woken up with a snake inside their sleeping bag or blanket because they were sleeping on the bare

ground without a tent to protect them. That'd be a very bad thing to have to go through. You'd have to

lie as still as possible until the creature tired of being there and crawled or slithered away. Yikes! That'd

be a very scary situation indeed. So, the next time you'll be sleeping in the great outdoors, be sure to

be in a tent with the flaps closed tight as you can get them.

Wood has been a very important thing for mankind over the centuries. Wood is sawn into lumber, and is Used to make paper. To make paper, a watery "soup" of cellulose wood fibers from the tree is mixed with lignin (A natural glue), water, and chemicals used in the pulping process. In ancient times, wood was used to make shelters and animal enclosures, etc. Crude boats such as dugout canoes were in use thousands of years ago. Later came canoes such as the American Indians made that had a wooden frame and either birch bark or animal hides stretched over them. The Indians used a type of pitch that came from tree sap and a couple of other ingredients mixed in. Wood has been a very popular material for the construction of homes all over the world. Wood particles and glue are used to make panels of wood such as plywood and particle board. These materials are commonly used in construction of houses, restaurants, and almost any building that can be conceived by the human mind. People build bird houses out wood, dog houses out of wood, skating rinks, fishing piers, lodges, ski chalets, and all sorts of structures. Wooden dowels are used in the construction of kites, pencils, skewers, corndog sticks, and even some types of arrows that are shot with target or hunting bows. Many target or hunting bows are made of wood, with some type of backing such as fiberglass or animal hide glued to them for strength. Furniture is often made of wood, and the forms that furniture can take are numerous because of the ability of wood to be molded and formed in so many ways. So, you see, wood is and always has been a very useful material to build or make things out of.

Music has always been a big part of people's lives. Even in the days before Christ gave his life on the cross at Calvary, music was being made by people for enjoyment and for religious purposes. People tapped out tunes on primitive drums, tapped on logs with sticks, and all sorts of things. Lyres, harps, and other musical instruments were created. I believe that someone began to pluck on a taut hunting bow string, and that was how the idea of creating a stringed musical instrument came into being. The lyre, the harp, and other instruments probably had their beginnings in the plucking of a bow string. Over the years, many more instruments were created. I have no doubt in the fact that the guitar is the most popular musical instrument in the world. The first guitars were derivatives of the lute, which is a stringed musical instrument that has an odd-looking body with a rounded back. The classical guitar was the first "real guitar" and had strings called cat gut strings. They were made of thin strips of cat gut. Of course, steel strings were later created and for the most part, steel strings are the most popular type used in modern music. There are steel string acoustic guitars, acoustic bass guitars, and electric bass guitars. Music has many facets. In the U.S.A., there is Bluegrass, Country, Blues, Rock, Gospel, Jazz, and other types of music. Music is a very wonderful thing, for the most part. Unless you are trying to sleep and someone has music blasting the speakers on a radio. Music is used as therapy in some cases. Music can be very soothing and enjoyable at times. What would a dance be like without music? What would a TV show or movie be like without background music. What would shopping be like without music? Music. We all love music.

Cats have been favorite pets for centuries. In the ancient tombs of the pharaohs, the mummified bodies of cats have been found. Cats were highly thought of back then, and they still are nowadays. The domesticated cats of today, are the descendants of the ancient cats. And even the wild cats such tigers, lions, panthers, and other cats are connected genetically somehow to the common domesticated house cat that eats at the feed bowl at your home. All cats are typically really good hunters of prey. They have the instinct to hunt for prey and prey usually fall victim to their skills. Some beautiful examples of the cat family are the bobcats. I have had the privilege of seeing these beautiful cats in the forest just twice so far in my life. The first one was pointed out to me by my paternal grandmother years ago as my granddaddy, my dad, and I were digging clay out of a creek bank for making pottery and bricks. It was a very pretty creature. My brother and I were fishing and floating down the river several years ago, when we saw a beautiful bobcat on the river bank. He saw the cats face, but a tree kept me from seeing the cats face. But what I could see of the animal was beautiful. Very beautiful. I love whenever a domesticated cat kneads on me. That is an ultimate way for a cat to show that it trusts you and likes you. I've had cats that played pretty- roughly with me. They'd go to scratching and even biting on me—

ha! That is fun. I like to play with a cat with a length of string and a piece of cloth attached to a stick.

Jesus Christ is the Savior of the world. I believe that there is no other name under heaven by which we may be saved. That is what the King James Bible says: Acts 4:12. Jesus of Nazareth. The King of Kings. The bright and morning star, The Rose of Sharon, The Savior (Or Saviour), The Lamb of God, and other names apply to him. The one and only Savior of the world. He turned water into wine, he raised the dead, he healed the blind and the lame, and those with infirmities. He was and still is the real deal. He cast out demons and people's lives were restored to full health and rightful minds. He still does those things, if only people will believe and have faith that he can. And he can. Yes, he can. He gave his life on the cross of Calvary so that everyone who would just believe would be able to escape the pits of hell and have everlasting life in the hereafter along with him and his father and the angels. Some people believe that anyone who believes in Jesus Christ and God the Father are crazy. But I believe, and no matter what the naysayers say, I will still believe in Jesus Christ, The Lamb of God. The healer, The Light of the world, He is the one and only way to be saved, according to the Christian faith. And I believe. Yes, I believe.

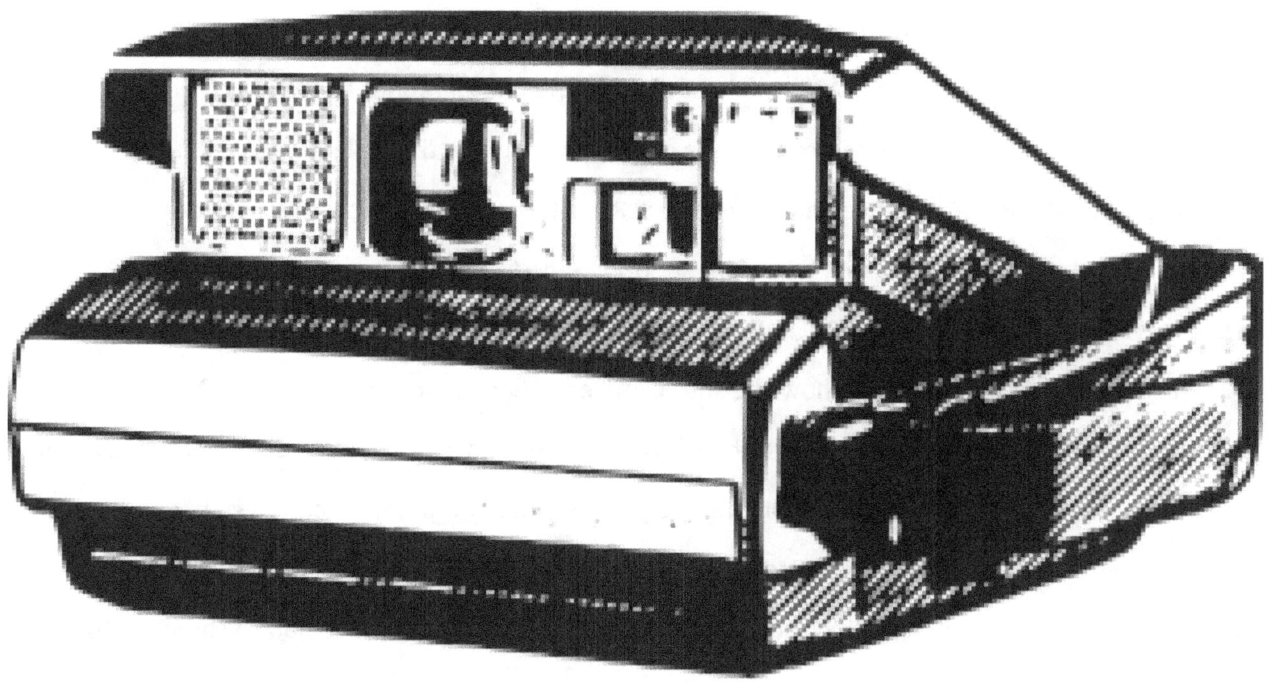

Photography is a very interesting thing to be involved in. The Camera Obscura was the device that

Started it all. Though he wasn't the very first man to use the Camera Obscura, a man named

Joseph Niepce used a portable Camera Obscura in the late 1830's in France to expose a pewter plate

coated with bitumen to light. That was the first image that didn't fade away quickly. Daguerreotypes,

Emulsion plates, and wet plates, were developed in the late 1800's. Richard Maddox improved upon

a previous invention and made dry gelatin plates that were nearly equal to wet plates in speed and

quality. They could be stored rather than made as needed. This gave photographers more freedom

in taking photographs. Cameras could be made smaller and handheld, instead of the bulky types

that were common in those days. Then George Eastman made cameras more accessible to everyone

when he started a company called Kodak in the 1880's. He created flexible roll film that didn't require

constant changing of solid plates. He invented a self-contained box camera that held 100 exposures.

It had a single lens and had no focusing adjustment. The user would take phots and send the camera

back to the Kodak company to be developed. It is very similar to the one-time use cameras in use today.

Around 1930, Henri Cartier Bresson and others began using 35mm rangefinder cameras. Bresson was

Known for capturing photos as life happened, instead of photos posed in a studio as many photographers were commonly doing those days. One of the best inventions in photography, was the Single Lens Reflex Camera (SLR). This type of camera allows the photographer to see what the image will be like before shooting the photo. With the Rangefinder, the photographer has to look through a view finder that is positioned slightly to one side of the actual image that will be taken. Rangefinders can be used to take some very nice photos, but an SLR is a little easier to focus and get your shot because you see what the image will be before shooting. And the most revolutionary creation in photography is the digital SLR or DSLR. With a DSLR, you can view what your photo will look like after each shot and if you don't like how the shot came out, then you can delete it and start over right then and there. And later you can do things to the photo to correct problems. This can be done in the camera, or in a photographic manipulating program on your computer. Technology has surely changed over the years, and for the better, I would say. The digital way, is the better way, in my humble opinion. Some do not agree with that, but it saves money that you would have had to spend on film and getting film processed. Film photography also has its merits, and some people wouldn't use a digital camera if they were given one. It's up to the photographer which type he or she prefers to use. Either way, photography is a very useful thing. So, go get your camera and take some photos. Who Knows? Maybe one of your photos will be deemed one of the prime examples of the photographic art.

Christmas is absolutely one of the most loved holidays in the world. In America, Christmas is a very big holiday. Some folks begin to decorate their homes a month in advance. They hang lights all along the eaves of their house, they start doing their Christmas gift shopping, and they send out colorful Christmas cards with whimsical designs on them. They begin to call friends and loved ones to discuss what they'll be doing for the holidays and to invite them to visit. A week or more before Christmas day, the ladies (And some of the fellows) will start baking cakes and pies, and other fine fare in preparation for the Christmas eve meal and the Christmas day meal. Oh, there'll be turkey, chicken, ham, dressing, potato salad, chicken and dumplings, turnip greens, baked cornbread and rolls, and other fine foods fixed to perfection and just waiting to be eaten by the families and friends. Oh, what a day. What a fine day. And after the Christmas meal, some like to take a nap, and some like to take a leisurely walk. Some like to sit around talking and laughing and watching TV. The night before Christmas, the children are told to get to bed early so that Santa and his reindeer can come to bring whatever gifts that Santa has decided is deserved by the children. So, the children go to bed with a heightened sense of anticipation. Surely for a while, they silently listen in hopes of hearing a sleigh and some hooves on the roof top, and maybe ol' Saint Nick trying to sneak around in the living room while placing gifts beneath the tree. Or maybe a little crunching on the cookies left for him. I do have memories of Christmas that are dear to me. Of family that I will never again see in this life. Of laughter and joking around and just plain fun. Christmas was a most enjoyable time for all of us back years ago, when we were all still alive and able to enjoy it. I still enjoy the season, though much has changed since those wonderful days when I was young. I remember how I would sit back and look at all the faces and see expressions of happiness on them. Bright smiles, all around. The gifts being unwrapped and the joy on the faces of those who received them and the ones who had given them. Usually there was a large stack of boxes both large and small under the tree. The angel or star brightly shined in the glow of the lights. Wonderful lights, that stood for something that we hoped would always be on Christmas. Beautiful Christmas. The birthday of our Lord and Savior. Or at least that was why we were celebrating the holiday, even if it wasn't the actual day of the year in which he was born. Jesus Christ. Savior of the world. Emmanuel. Christmas is the time that we celebrate his birth.

Birds of all kinds are present all over the world. There are tiny birds and large birds and birds that are medium-sized. Some birds are so small, that they don't even weigh an ounce. Some humming birds fall into that category. On the upper end of the spectrum, birds like emus and ostriches are quite large. Now extinct, the Dodo, was a large flightless bird that lived on the island of Mauritius, east of Madagascar in the Indian ocean. It was first seen around 1598, and sailors hunted the birds to extinction. They were last seen in 1662. The emu and the ostrich are also large flightless birds. The ostrich is the larger of the two. Finches are tiny birds and can be seen sitting on brush piles and other things that they can perch on. Finches are commonly seen at bird feeders. Red Cardinals and blue jays are also common sights at feeders. The blue jays love to eat acorns and have been credited with spreading oak trees around North America over the centuries. Many times, I have seen blue jays chase other birds away from a feeder. A bird that was standing at the feeder suddenly got chased off when a blue jay landed on the feeder. Red cardinals do their best to intimidate other male cardinals that are in the area. Male cardinals typically are brighter red in color, while the female doesn't look quite as pretty. The female has a different and somewhat duller coloration than the male. I have seen tiny hummingbirds getting chased away from a hummingbird feeder by a slightly-larger hummingbird of a different coloration. We laughed when the slightly -larger bird swooped down and chased the smaller bird away. The smaller bird would come back to the feeder in a few minutes, and the larger bird would swoop down from its perch again and chase the smaller bird away. It was comical to see, for sure. I remember one time as I sat in the doorway of my home reading the bible, a small bird of some kind landed on my leg and sat there for a couple seconds before flying away. I was surprised, to say the least. And I wondered if it was a sign from heaven above. Who knows? Not I. But I sure would like to think of it that way.

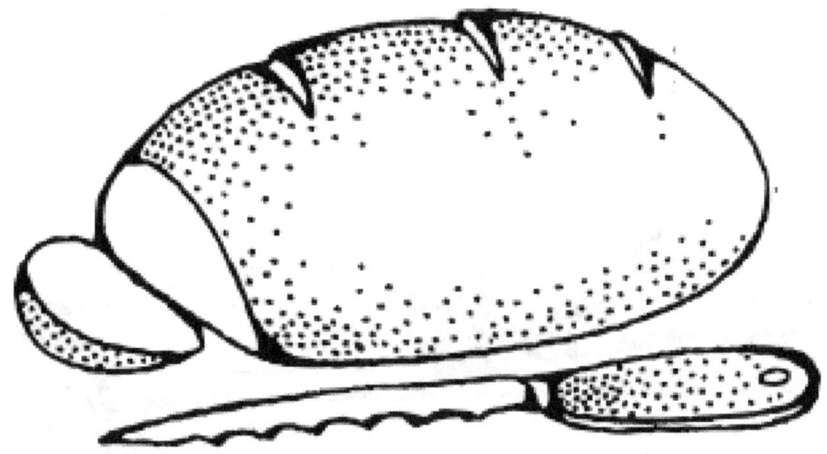

Food. "Man doth not live by bread alone." Says one verse in the bible. Men and women surely love to eat. Everyone enjoys eating. It is one of the joys of life. Of course, the bible verse mentioned wasn't exactly talking about the food people eat or the act of eating. It was talking of the spiritual food that people need. But, while people are alive on this earth, they have to have nourishment to survive. All sorts of foods exist. I remember as a child, we would get up in the morning and wait for breakfast to be prepared. I remember the smell of bacon and eggs being fried. I remember grits boiling in a pot and butter on a butter dish just waiting to be put in those grits along with the eggs. And sometimes we would have stacks of pancakes along with syrup and butter. On cold mornings, my grandmother would make a large pot full of hot chocolate. We surely loved that hot chocolate. I wish that I had a hot cup of that right now. Lordy Mighty, that was good stuff. I remember really- good meals with such goodies as fried chicken, field peas, corn on the cob, corn bread, sweet potatoes, turnip greens, and mashed potatoes and gravy. And for dessert, we would have some kind of cake, pie, or pudding.

I really enjoy eating Chinese food, and go to Chinese restaurants every now and again. I also like to cook a steak or hamburger meat on a barbecue grill. I like to put barbecue sauce on the meat right before the meat is ready to be taken off the grill. Then I toast the buns or light bread on the grill. One of the tastiest things that I ever ate that came off a grill, was corn on the cob that was put in some tinfoil with some butter and spices and cooked for a while. Man, that was really tasty. One of the best-tasting "Store-Bought" foods that I ever purchased and ate, was something called Chicken Cordon Bleau. Lordy mighty, that stuff tastes amazing. Really good! "Food is what makes the world go round." Someone might say. And no one would probably disagree with them. Especially if hungry.

Tools have been in use for ages upon ages. In the bible, tools were mentioned. Men used tools to build boats, and structures of various kinds. The bible mentions how men would make various kinds of vessels for sacrifices, etc. In the 1800's in America, men would go out into the forests and cut down trees with long crosscut saws. And they had pits dug into the ground that would allow a man to stand in the pit and saw from below the log while a man on top of the pit would hold the handle on the other end of the saw. This was really- labor-intensive work and some say that men back then were tougher than men of today. I do believe that the men of those bygone ages were conditioned to do more physical work than men nowadays. I believe that education and technology has had a lot to do with that. Both of my Granddaddy's were involved in the logging industry at one time. They told me about the Hard work that they did back in their younger days. It didn't just sound like tough work. It was tough work! And the pay wasn't great either. My dad's dad told me how he had to chop three cords of wood to buy his first guitar. That guitar probably cost just a few dollars, and he had to cut three loads of wood with an axe to be able to purchase it. Now that was wanting a guitar. That was definitely determination. My granddaddy (Same one) was also a wood worker and potter and he made some of his own tools for wood working and pottery. He even made his own pottery wheel and he built a brick making machine to build the bricks on his home. They are some of the most beautiful bricks that I have ever seen. We used to go down to the creeks and dig clay with grubbing hoes (Mattocks) for his pottery and the bricks. Tools have played a big part in our lives. We had brick-toting tools, digging tools, shovels, pipe wrenches, saws of various types, hammers of various types, plumb bobs, levels, squares, screwdrivers, ratchets, sockets, and various types of shop tools such as band saws, drill presses, and lathes. Tools surely can come in handy in life. Especially for craftsmen like my granddaddy Mosley used to be.

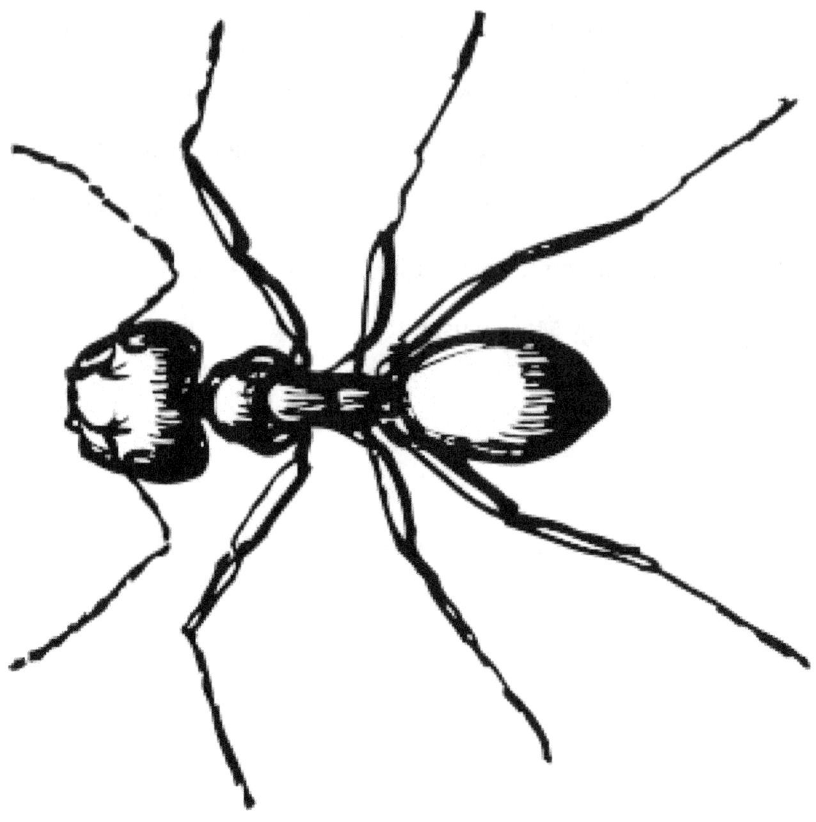

Insects. There are many types of insects in the world. The world is literally covered with these creatures. Ants, dragon flies, cicadas, butterflies, mosquitos, house flies, mantis, yellow jackets, honey bees, bumble bees, carpenter bees, fleas, earwigs, termites, fireflies, hornets, lady bugs, crickets, cow ants, grasshoppers, mayflies, beetles, aphids, horseflies, cockroaches, meal worms, and weevils are just some of the numerous types of insects that cover the earth. There are many more types. One of the most desired products from the insect population is honey. People all over the world treasure this sweet product that bees produce. Many people use honey as an alternative to sugar in their food and drinks. People like to put honey in cereal, coffee, and even iced tea. It is also placed into and onto cakes, cookies, and other treats. I like to go to the county fair to walk around and see the exhibits. There usually is a couple there selling candy that they buy that has honey inside of it. I usually buy some of the candy and really enjoy it. It tastes good, and is flavored like different kinds of fruit. During times when it has rained a lot, the ants will bite the heck out of folks who are unfortunate enough to cross their path. I have fallen victim to their tormenting stings on more than one occasion. Another torturous thing is when horse flies and deer flies bite. The sting of the horse fly is the most torturous of the two, but both can make being out of doors miserable during the summer and spring. Mosquitos are really-pesky critters also. They are usually present on most summer days and have a tendency to attack a person relentlessly in their quest for a meal of blood. I was raised on a farm and when we went into the corn crib, we often saw tiny weevils that had gotten into the corn sacks or in the sacks of grain that we used to feed the hogs. Cotton weevils often get in the cotton bolls. That is why they are called Boll Weevils. Some of the most-hated insect critters in the world are roaches. There are small German roaches, and larger cockroaches. Both are pests that need to be eradicated from the face of the earth (In my humble opinion). They will get into everything in the house if left to their own devices. Nasty. Just plain nasty. Some of the most-beloved insects in the world, are butterflies. Butterflies are for the most part, some of the most beautiful creatures that the Good Lord ever created. They can be seen alighting on flowers wherever flowers can be found. They alight and begin to eat the nectar of the flower. While they are eating the nectar, they often move their wings in an up and down motion. They are absolutely-beautiful creatures, for the most part. Some are yellow and black. Some are orange and black. And some are other colors. Who doesn't love to see a beautiful butterfly on a flower? I know of no one who doesn't. Absolutely no one.

Sports. Mankind has always enjoyed participating in and watching various types of sports. In America, and Canada, the Indians played many types of games. One of the most popular games was manataka (Lacrosse). The French gave manataka the name Lacrosse. Another game that they played was a game that involved shooting arrows at a hoop as it rolled across the ground. It was called the hoop and pole game. (I am not sure about why it was called hoop and pole game, because it didn't involve a pole, unless a pole was used to keep the hoop moving. Maybe it was? Since ancient times, wrestling and foot races have been sports that folks have enjoyed watching and participating in. Back in the 1800's, folks would step into burlap sacks or other kinds of sacks and race toward a finish line. Another funny race was when two folks would stand side-by-side and tie the two legs in the middle together with a strip of cloth or string and then they would work together to be the first people over the finish line. Naturally, it was a spectacle for sure, and some would trip and fall down and would have to get up and try to get going again. Baseball and softball was played in communities by church teams or community teams back in the 1800's. I used to enjoy playing softball in local community games and I always loved the smell of a new leather glove. That's a wonderful smell rhat always brings back memories. Catching the ball was exciting and hitting the ball out into the field was a blast. I always enjoyed playing soccer and volleyball. Soccer was filled with action. I have a big toe that was driven in as result of being kicked twice by the same fellow who was trying to block me from kicking the ball. I was taken immediately to the hospital for x-rays and all that goes with it. Games of volleyball were action-packed also, and took skill to win points. I went out for football, but had trouble getting a ride to practice and quit after a short while. I never was really into the idea of playing football anyhow, and was basically being pushed into it by my dad who totally enjoyed the sport when he was in high school. He still watches football on TV and goes to football games when he can. I never watch sports on TV or go to games anymore. I have had other interests that have held more weight in life, such as playing music, writing songs and stories, metal detecting/treasure hunting, and creating artwork. But I've got memories of playing sports and don't regret doing so.

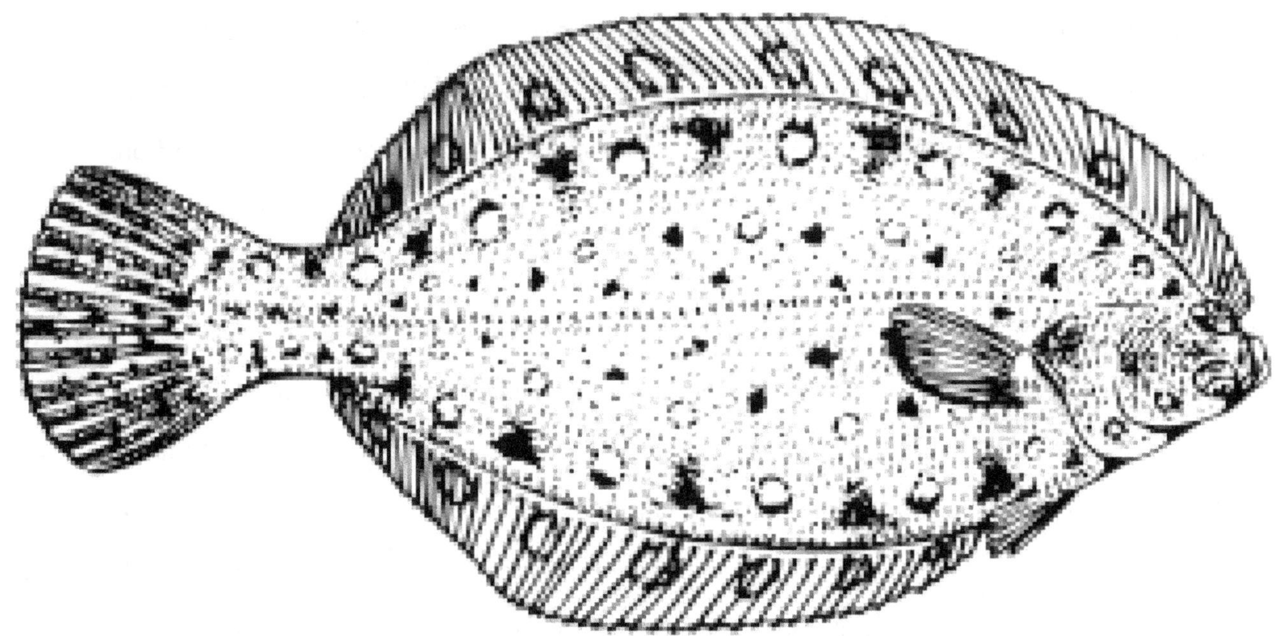

Fish. Fish live in rivers, streams, ponds, lakes, bays, oceans, seas, and sometimes aquariums and fish

bowls. Fish live in underground caves, in canals, and other places as well. Fish are eaten by mankind,

and wild and domesticated animals. Fish is one of the most popular resources of meat in the world.

For centuries, men have gone out on the water to cast nets and to let out their baited hooks in hopes

of catching fish. In my opinion, one of the best stories that I have ever read was "The Old Man and the

Sea." Written by famed author, Ernest Hemingway. It truly is a fine story. There is a story in the bible

about some men who were catching nothing after several casts of their net. And Jesus told them to cast

their net on the other side of the boat and they did so and were totally surprised when they caught so

many fish that they could barely haul their net in. That is a wonderful story also. Probably the best of all

considering who was making it possible. Jesus, was the master of fishing and was a "Fisher of men."

In small ponds, I have seined for crayfish and minnows in the past. While doing so, I have also caught a

few fish such as small bream, catfish, and jackfish. We used to catch what we called "Pollywogs." Which

was a type of small catfish that lived in the creeks and streams and mostly had to be caught at night on

limb lines in the deep holes of the creeks or streams. We used chicken gizzards and chicken liver to catch

them. I've heard about folks putting chunks of soap on hooks and catching catfish also. I tried it, but

didn't have any luck doing so. Fishermen have used soap in fish boxes to catch catfish also, but I've

never used a box trap. My stepdad did and had some luck, but due to back trouble, he gave up using boxes and has used trout lines (Some folks call them "Trot Lines.") ever since and is getting up in age and has decided that his trout line fishing days are over (Or almost over) because of the safety issues at his advanced age. He took an elderly friend fishing with him several years ago and the friend fell out of the boat and he said that he had a terrible time helping him get back into the boat. And for a while, the friend would ask to be taken back fishing on the river, but my stepdad refused to do so because he knew that if he fell out of the boat again, he would probably not be able to help him get back into the boat like he did before. It's sad, but it is also a wise decision for my stepdad to make. He is not as strong as he was just a few years back, and age is taking its toll. I enjoy fishing for flounder, though I haven't fished for them in several years. I used to go by a bait shop and buy a dozen minnows or a little more and take them to a rocky area by the road where folks like to fish for them. I had a little luck on some days, and on some days the fish just wouldn't be biting. I caught two nice-sized flounders (One at one location, and the other somewhere else many miles away) while using my dad's idea. The idea was to use a strip of salt meat to jig around in the water near a canal bank. I did so, and caught a pretty nice flounder. On the other occasion, I was fishing off a pier. This summer I made two simple flounder lights that I hoped to use, but skin cancer problems kept me out of the water and I decided to wait until next season to try my luck. I have never gigged a flounder, but went with my dad, my brother, and cousins a few times years ago when I was a teenager. My dad gigged 17 flounders one night years ago when he was younger. I have fished a few times for bream in the last couple years. I enjoy fishing for bream and seeing the cork bobbing up and down in the water whenever a fish strikes the bait. One of the best reasons that I fished for bream over the last several years, was that my mother and stepdad liked to fry them up and we'd eat them for dinner at their house. When she passed away from ALS, it kind of killed my joy of fishing and still isn't totally something that I care much about anymore. Sure, I enjoy catching a fish, but the true joy of fishing so that I could bring the fish back and clean them for our mid-day meal is gone forever. My stepdad doesn't worry about cooking too much anymore. With mom gone, why bother cooking a meal when eating at a restaurant or microwaving something quick to fix will do the trick—so to speak. My brother is into bass fishing and has been fishing for them for years in tournaments and just for the fun of it. Yes, he knows what color plastic worm or what plug will get the best results in nearly every situation. As I said, flounders have always been one of my favorite fishes. And there's nothing quite as tasty as a piece of flounder meat that is cooked just right.

Musical instruments. For ages upon ages people have made music with all sorts of musical instruments.

They have banged on drums, they have strummed and plucked the strings of harps. They have played

lutes, guitars (Classical and steel stringed types), banjos, mandolins, fiddles(Violins), etc. Classical guitars

used to be strung with catgut strings. Later nylon strings were developed and have long since been

in use on classical guitars. Steel stringed acoustic guitars are more commonly used by musicians who

play acoustic guitars. I play acoustic guitar and like either a nylon strung guitar or a steel string guitar.

Both have their merits and both are more suited to the style of music for which they have most

commonly been used for. Electric guitars are very popular also. In today's music scene, you will most

likely encounter someone playing an electric guitar. Electric guitars can be changed by switches and

knobs so that the sound can vary greatly as one plays and adjusts the switches and knobs. Of course,

the amplifier has a lot to do with the sound of an electric guitar. The settings of an amp can vary

greatly and can allow a guitarist to sound differently according to how the settings on the amp are

adjusted. Bass guitars thump out a beat and work in conjunction with the drummer of a band to

keep the timing of the music going. There are acoustic basses like the large standup type used by the musicians in the fifties, and acoustic basses that are about the size of an acoustic guitar, and there are electric basses that are made of a solid piece of wood in much the same way that most electric guitars are made. And I have seen simple homemade single string basses that are nothing more than a taught string attached to the end of a broom stick that is attached to a big washtub. The string is attached to the washtub on the lower end and attached to the top end of the broom stick. The washtub acts like a sound box when the string is plucked. Thump! Thump! Thump! And everybody smiles and chuckles. What could be more comical? But it works. It definitely works. Harmonicas have long been a favorite musical instrument. I enjoy the metal detecting hobby and I find the reeds from harmonicas at nearly every old home site that I search at. One reason these musical instruments were so popular over the years, was that they were very cheap instruments. They were a nice little gift for someone that didn't cost much and they would allow a person to entertain themselves and others. Remember, years ago there were no radios, TV's, computers, or other means to entertain yourself. You, or someone else, had to do the entertaining and most folks couldn't afford a piano. So, the harmonica was a good and reasonably-priced way for someone to make music and be entertained. Musical instruments such as bugles, trumpets, saxophones, and flutes all have been popular in music as well. Who doesn't like to hear a person playing some kind of musical instrument? I know that I enjoy hearing someone who can play an instrument well. That can be very nice. Very nice, indeed.

Animals have been living on the earth for a very long time. There are many species and types of animals living on earth and some that were living on earth and now are extinct. Dodo birds once lived and thrived on the Island of Mauritius, but due to being hunted by sailors back in the 1600's, they became extinct. Mice and rats have been around for a very long time also. Archaeologists have found evidence of their presence in diggings. The evidence was very old in some cases. Cats have been around a long time also. Cat remains have been found in the tombs of the pharaohs. Cats were highly-revered as pets back in the days when the pharaohs were living in Egypt. Of course, dogs have always been favored as pets. I have always preferred having cats as pets, but some people don't feel as I do about them. I try to spoil mine rotten—ha! I love those critters. Just love them. My maternal grandmother must have owned a hundred or more dogs over the years. I joked with her and told her that if she were to win the lotto, she'd probably build a dog house that'd stretch all the way to California. My grandmother also had a pet skunk, some raccoons, a pair of ferrets, and rabbits. It was like living on Old Macdonald's Farm around there. Goats, hogs, horses, chickens, turkeys, cows, burros, and cats and dogs. All sorts of creatures lived on my grandparent's farm in the country.

One good thing about raising chickens, is there usually is a fresh supply of eggs to be had. And one good thing about being raised on a farm, is that there is a fresh supply of bacon and souse after butchering day. We would do the butchering of the hogs on a cold winter morning. "Hog Head Cheese" was made from the head of the hog. Chitterlings (We pronounced them "Chitlins") were the cleaned-out intestines of the hog that would be fried in cooking grease until they were golden brown. Pork chops, and other cuts of meat were made from the hog. Those were some of the memories I have of being raised on a southern farm. I find it hard to believe that I actually ate Chitterlings ("Chitlins"). When I think of it now, it seems nasty. Plain old nasty. After all, we know what was in those hog intestines just before they were "Cleaned." Yuck! Double Yuck! And as I recall the experience years ago, I can remember that they tasted a bit like what was inside them before the "Cleaning"……..ha! Animals do have a purpose on this earth, even though I have- to wonder why some of them were created. Such as deadly poisonous snakes that could kill us with one strike, or fierce lions and tigers that would kill a human in short order if given half a chance. Or sharks that would bite a person in-two in a snap second in salty bodies of water (And it has happened in fresh water in the past). But it is not what I think about the existence of those creatures that matters. God wanted them to exist. Therefore, they exist. Period!

www.ingramcontent.com/pod-product-compliance
Lightning Source LLC
Chambersburg PA
CBHW080815280726
48660CB00018B/3455